WHEN
WERE ALWAYS
BLUE

Memories of
a Lewes boyhood

W.F. Wells

© Sheila Wells 2004

Edited by Joy Preston

Published in 2004 for The Friends of Lewes Society by Pomegranate Press
51 St Nicholas Lane, Lewes, Sussex BN7 2JZ
email: pomegranatepress@aol.com
website: pomegranate-press.co.uk

ISBN 0-9542587-9-7

British Library Cataloguing-in-Publication Data.
A catalogue record for this book is available from the British Library.

Printed by rpm print & design, 2–3 Spur Road, Quarry Lane Industrial Estate, Chichester, West Sussex PO19 8PR

FOREWORD

William Frederick (Bill) Wells, who died in 1983, wrote this memoir of his boyhood in the mid–1970s, after his retirement. He also, with his remarkable memory for visual detail, drew the accompanying illustrations of his old home at 12 West Street, Lewes.

In 2003 Mr Wells's widow, Mrs Sheila Wells, sent the memoir in manuscript to the Friends of Lewes to see if the Society would be interested in publishing it. It was indeed interested, and this book is the result. We are very grateful to Mrs Wells for all her help.

CONTENTS

1

THE BEGINNING

The way of life I knew as a boy has vanished, probably forever. In my boyhood we had no television or telephone, radio or refrigerator, central heating or electric light. Life was unhurried and kept time with the seasons. Summers were summers, hot and blazing, and winter froze the brooks and whitened the Downs. Mine was a carefree childhood, and I led a healthy outdoor life, running and roaming freely over the hills and through the woods which cradled the town.

The woods were places of mystery, alive with birds and small animals, but those undulating hills, those grey-green oceans of grassland, free of fence or ditch, were our joy. There we were unrestricted and unrestrained, able to run and romp over the close-cropped turf, chasing and playing for hours in the crisp clean air under a sky that seemed always blue. Each day was an adventure in learning. Trying and testing, experimenting and experiencing, observing and memorising, so that now every street and stream, field and farm, recalls some memory of my early years. My boyhood recollections are now more sharp and vivid than events of later years.

My home was a small country town, where you not only knew everybody, but remembered them fifty years later. People knew and cared about you, they dropped in unannounced and stayed to tea or supper, and we did the same. We were a society where everyone knew, or knew of, everybody else, where newcomers were befriended and quickly became part of the communal life of the town. Most of the community had lived all their lives in the ancient houses and cottages that lined the hilly streets of the Borough. They had never moved far from their homes. Although no more than seven miles from the sea, which could be seen from the higher parts of the town, to many the seaside was a remote and alien land.

Much was made of an outing to the coast, as much as we today make of an African safari coupled with a few days on some tropic island. It was a homelier town in those days, quieter and cosier, smelling of wood smoke and horse dung, blossoms and brewing. The peace of its streets had not yet been ravaged by the motorcar, and the air was as yet unpolluted by petrol and diesel fumes.

I was born at four o'clock in the afternoon of January the twelfth, 1909, in the huge brass bedstead which dominated the largest of the rooms on the first floor of our home in West Street. This was the house where my grandfather began and developed his business, and where my parents had lived since their marriage in 1904.

A doctor by the name of Steinhauser, he later changed it to Stenhouse, brought me into the world, and when I was a few months old he removed two fleshy growths from the crown of my head, using the kitchen as an operating theatre. One naevus he cut away, the other he burnt, by what means I do not know, but all my life I have borne the mark of the burning. The hair has never grown naturally around the scar, but is obstinate, and sprouts at peculiar angles, making it difficult to groom and keep tidy. As a boy my unruly hair annoyed my father but Mother, more tolerant, joked about it, saying my head was like heaven as there was no parting there. A nurse, with the unusual name of Hogsflesh, assisted the doctor, and I believe attended my mother at my birth. I remember her well, but how old I was when her rugged face first registered in my mind I do not know. Perhaps she had been called to deal with some childish disorder, but I can still see her bending over me. Perhaps it was the tufted hair on the chin of that kindly countenance that has indelibly printed her features in my memory.

Measles, mumps and chickenpox I caught and recovered from at an early age. It was an accepted fact that children at some time would have these illnesses and that it was advisable to have them in youth rather than later. I escaped the more serious complications of these complaints, and the infectious and contagious diphtheria and scarlet fever outbreaks which from time to time menaced the townsfolk. The 'fever cart' was a common sight about the town. This was a boxlike, horse-drawn carriage with curtained windows, in which the blanketed patient was conveyed in a sitting position to the isolation hospital for treatment.* I remember none of the discomforts of my childish ailments, but I do remember the convalescence. The enticing food to tempt the appetite, books and comics to amuse, and being allowed to sit before the bedroom fire, wrapped in dressing-gown and feet in carpet slippers, listening to Mother reading or telling a story. Sitting cosy and warm in the candlelight, watching the dancing flames and twinkling sparks of the glowing coals.

My mother was rarely ill, but I remember an occasion when she must have been gravely so, for a Nurse Fisher occupied the dressing-room adjoining my parents' bedroom. I was told that my mother 'had a quinsy'. Not knowing that this was an illness, when allowed to see her, I expected to find some strange creature in her bed, but Mother reassured me, saying she had not been well, and allayed my fears.

My boyhood was healthy, free from accident and illness, until shortly before my fourteenth birthday, when stomach pains were diagnosed as a grumbling appendix. It was then fashionable to have one's appendix removed, and the doctor, leaving an apprehensive boy in bed and an agitated mother to pack pyjamas, left to arrange for the operation to be performed at the local cottage hospital. After a few days, I got up, Mother unpacked, and I'm still waiting to hear from the hospital. I don't expect to hear from the doctor as he died over thirty years ago.

The isolation hospital was opposite Nevill Crescent on the other side of Nevill Road. St Mary's Social Centre now occupies the building.

No 12 West Street (see also page 50)

2

NO. 12, WEST STREET

The Façade

Three holystoned steps, set in an arched recess, led up from the red brick pavement to the green-painted front door. These steps, worn hollow by countless feet, were now stepped over rather than on, since whitening them had become the fashion. Most visitors and the family used the side door, which at pavement level opened into a wide passage, where brick steps at its far end led up to a small paved yard at the back of the house. This passageway had once housed builders' paraphernalia before my grandfather bought the land for the Market Lane workshop. I have always understood, but have not been able to confirm, that a previous owner of No 12 was a milkman. He used this passage as a dairy, and it was rumoured that he hung himself from a hook in the ceiling, above which was my bedroom. The story never prevented us from enjoying the many games we devised and played in this covered way, or caused me any sleepless nights. In fact Father added another hook to the one in the beam and from them suspended a swing, which gave us endless pleasure.

The upper panels of the front door were glazed with leaded lights of brightly coloured glass, between which was a brass knocker of huge proportions, matching the large brass door knob and the equally large letterbox. Bold black Roman capitals engraved in its brass surround proclaimed this to be the house of W. WELLS, BUILDER. The cleaning of this brazen furniture, and the sweeping and swilling down of the pavement, was one of my regular tasks. The whitening of the steps was Mother's preserve. Sometimes Mother delegated the whitening of the steps to my sister. It was never given to me. Perhaps it was considered not to be boys' work, but I do remember being sent to Bridgmans, the stone masons, to buy a piece of Bathstone for the purpose. This was before step powder in tins was found to be more convenient and efficient. I believe in the days before the war this was the duty of the current maid. I remember well one young girl, Jennie Stephens, whose main task was to look after my sister and myself. She was gentle and kind, and I remember now our sorrow when Mother told us she would not be coming again. She had died of consumption.

Jennie was no doubt engaged as a maid before I was born, as an incident occurred when I was a few weeks old that has been retold with much amusement by members of the family throughout the years. It was told to me again quite recently by my cousin, who is older than I and remembers the occasion. I had been given my morning bottle, and left tucked up and fast asleep in my parents' bed. Sent upstairs to see if all was well, the girl rushed down in panic, crying that I had gone. I was not in or under the bed or anywhere in the room.

'Gone, he can't have gone, he can't walk,' Mother replied. In the sparsely furnished room there was no obvious hiding place. It was said that they pulled out and emptied the drawers of the chest and opened the wardrobe doors in this search, but I suspect this was an elaboration of the tale as it was retold. I was eventually found fast asleep, wedged between the mattress and the wall, unaware of the commotion I had caused by my sudden disappearance. The incident acted as a spur to Father, who quickly finished the high-sided cot he was making and had not been able to complete by the time of my arrival, which was a little early.

The Parlour

The front door opened upon a narrow passage, facetiously referred to as the 'hall'. Its narrowness was further reduced by a coat rack and a cast iron umbrella stand. On one's left as one entered this hall was the front room, a room where visitors were entertained and where we on Sundays sat with our books or played our less boisterous games.

As a choir boy I attended three, sometimes four, services each Sunday, which left little time for relaxation in this cosy parlour. An aspidistra in a jardinière on an ebonised table, a whatnot with its china, the alcoved shelves of books and bric-à-brac, and the bobble-trimmed pelmet of the shelf supporting the many-mirrored overmantel, gave the room an air of Edwardian gentility.

Here of an evening, the day's work finished, Mother would sit, with knitting or needlework. Sometimes alone, at others with an aunt or one of her many friends. In summer she would sit behind the billowing curtains, elevated above the bustle of the street, and watch the folk and the life of the town as it passed below. In the hottest weather it was the coolest room in the house, but with the lower sash open for ventilation it was the dustiest. When I was a boy, most of the traffic was horse-drawn and the road surface was uneven and flinty, not the smooth tarmacked street of today. In the summer, the sprinklers of the horse-drawn water-cart cooled its surface and laid its dust, and occasionally it was tarred and sanded. It was at these times that Mother had no complaints of the dust from the road pervading the front room. In winter she had no such problem. With curtains drawn, logs blazing in the cast iron black-leaded grate, flames mirrored in the tiled surround and glinting on the brass fender, the room was cosy and warm.

The parlour

The old Sunday evenings, with Winter outside
And hymns in the front room, the piano our guide.

Full use was never made of the piano which dominated the room. Although she was not able to play herself, this musical monstrosity was Mother's pride and joy. It was dusted and polished until its fretted front, brass brackets and veneered vulgarity shone and reflected the flickering firelight of a winter's day. Its huge bulk occupied almost the entire side of the room opposite the window, leaving just sufficient room for a chair with a tapestry-covered seat in the corner by the door, and a small armchair in the alcove by the fire. On the distempered wall, above the family photographs in varied frames on the piano's polished top, hung an oil painting of a thatched cottage in a country lane. This was another treasured possession of Mother's. It is now hanging above my fireplace. I know nothing of its history, but I like to think that my great-grandparents enjoyed, as much as I, the peaceful English scene the nineteenth century artist has depicted.

My sister was given piano lessons but had little aptitude and did not reach a very high standard of playing. It was the fashion of that era for girls to be taught to play, but it was not considered a suitable accomplishment for boys. I regret not being given the opportunity, but no doubt my training as a chorister was thought sufficient for my musical education. It was chiefly friends vamping the songs and tunes of the times or others, more accomplished, playing popular classics and sacred songs, who entertained us on Sunday evenings, at parties, and on special family celebrations.

The Kitchen
At the foot of the narrow stairs, which were the same width as and a continuation of the hall, a panelled door on the left opened into what was always referred to as the 'kitchen'. This bay-windowed room was the hub of the house. It was also the home of the table. This massive piece of mahogany monopolised the tiny room. Its size was the bane of Mother's life, but its sturdy construction saved her from serious injury when in 1940

the house was damaged by a bomb dropped by a hit-and-run German plane. An ornately carved walnut marble-topped chiffonier made negotiation of the monster's northern side difficult, but the bay-windowed recess gave one more space to pass along its southern edge, to reach the easy chairs each side of the red-tiled, copper-kettled hearth and black-leaded grate.

I clearly remember the grotesque eagle, which surmounted the chiffonier's curiously carved mirror frame, falling off its perch at the outbreak of war. It was regarded as an omen. Good or bad I do not know, but it was never replaced. A wall mirror, in a gilded pillared frame above the fireplace, reflected a copper warming-pan and old prints of the town hanging on the match-boarded partition, screening the stairs to the bedrooms and the stone steps to the cellar. This glass, and the mirrored doors and overmantel of the chiffonier, contrived to lighten and enlarge the room. The bay window of the kitchen looked out upon a small brick-paved yard.

The kitchen

To the left were steps leading down into the side passage, above which was a workshop at garden level. Opposite the window, five York stone steps led up to this garden, and to the right of the yard was the scullery. Only in summer was the sun high enough in orbit for it to appear above the surrounding buildings and its rays reach the room. It was mostly reflected light from the regularly white-washed walls of the workshop and wash-house, that brightened the otherwise dim interior of the kitchen.

The Scullery

Through the other match-boarded door one entered the scullery. This was a domestic workshop, a utility room, making use of every inch of the plastered walls and red brick floor of the narrow, low-ceilinged cell. Compact, and crowded with purpose-made, cunningly contrived, painted pine racks, shelves and cupboards, it was a manually operated equivalent of modern electric elegance.

A pine dresser, stained and grained to imitate mahogany, made the most of its cramped corner to the right of the kitchen door. Decorated with domestic china, cups on hooks, plates in racks, caddies and canisters – their tight tin lids protecting the contents from the steamy atmosphere – drawers of linen and cutlery, cupboards crammed with pots and pans of glass and earthenware, it was conveniently placed for the easy setting of the kitchen table for meals, and for the reception of the washed crockery after.

Curtained shelves concealed boots and shoes, and a nest of drawers accommodated cleaning materials and miscellanea necessary for the smooth running of the house. Wall shelves of various widths supported pans of different depths and diameters for use on the range in the recess at the far end of the scullery, and a copper in the corner to the left of the range supplied hot water on Monday for the weekly wash and on Saturday night for the family baths.

Behind a match-boarded door to the right of the range was the toilet. As the house was built on a bank, the ground rose steeply at the back. Consequently this small room was partially underground. Only a small amount of daylight, from a tiny pane of obscure glass set high up in the rear

The scullery

wall, penetrated this narrow cell. As this window was at ground level outside, it was often obscured by garden growth, which gave an eerie green tinge to the twilight of the toilet. There was no gas jet or light bulb to lighten the gloom, only the flickering flame of a candle in an enamelled holder on a minute shelf relieved its claustrophobic atmosphere. Beneath this shelf, on a loop of string, hung the toilet paper – six-inch squares of newspaper. I remember the size as it was one of my tasks to ensure that there was always an adequate supply. So narrow was the toilet that the introduction and fixing by Father of a wooden holder for a toilet roll considerably reduced the space for one to manoeuvre. As it was partially underground, moisture penetrated the brickwork and dampened the plaster-rendered walls.

Although frequently decorated, large areas of paint would peel away, revealing a stained surface beneath. Although dim and dark, being next to the kitchen range it was cosy and warm. The majority of houses of that period had primitive outside closets. Ours, being inside, was much appreciated by the family and visitors on dark and wintry nights.

The Cellar

One's passage from the hall, through the kitchen to the scullery, was slightly impeded by the warming-pan and the prints on the staircase partition. A curtain hanging on brass rings from a wooden pole, angled across the corner to lessen draughts from the scullery and cellar, further complicated one's entry or exit, particularly as the doors to these two places were hinged so as to open into the kitchen.

Behind the cellar door, on painted shelves fixed to the whitewashed wall, was Mother's pantry of perishable foods. Cheese and butter in covered dishes, opened pots of jam and paste, cold meat and bacon under miniature gauze umbrellas, were kept fresh by the cool air ascending the flight of well worn stone steps that led to the dim depths below. On the brick floor below the shelves in a large earthenware crock, with the bread board for a lid, the loaves remained fresh and crisp. Beside this crock, in a smaller edition of a milkman's churn, or sometimes in a jug, covered with a square of muslin weighted with beads at the corners, the milk kept sweet and cool even in the hottest weather.

The narrow-steps needed frequent cleaning, for one could not avoid trampling the dust when carrying fuel from the cellar. Each year sufficient coal was stored to last the winter through. It would arrive by horse-drawn wagon, sometimes bagged, sometimes loose. However careful the coalman, dust covered everything. Those lumps of Derby brights which were too large to pass down the chute in the pavement had to be carried through the side passage to the cellar and then stacked to form a retaining wall for the smaller pieces.

When all was stored, the clean-up began. Mother swept and whitened the front step and, before I was old enough to do it, a labourer from the workshop would swill down the passageway and scrub the front pavement. Much the same procedure was followed when the logs arrived, though the task was not so dirty. I never knew the quantity Father ordered, but often it needed two huge farm horses to draw the heavy wagon of oak logs. These were off-loaded on the road and pavement close to the side door. There was very little traffic to impede by doing so, but we worked like beavers to get the bulky load through the doorway into the passage as quickly as possible. Then under cover, and at our leisure, we stacked the load as neatly as possible at the far end, where we could draw upon the pile to fuel the open fires of the house.

Kindling wood was also stored in the passageway. Here at a very early age I was taught by my father to use a saw. Lengths of old floorboard and similar waste from the carpenter's shop I would first examine for nails and remove if found. Then with pencil and try square I would mark lines six and three quarter inches apart, this being the length that fitted the open grate and the kitchen range. If they were longer the barred front of the range would not close, but why the pieces had to be so exact for the open fires I do not know. However, it was an excellent exercise in accuracy. It taught me to saw true to a line, and to estimate a measurement to within a sixteenth of an inch. The pieces when cut were stacked hard against the wall, so that any that deviated from the length would show when my labour was checked. When all the waste had been cut and stacked, it needed little effort with an axe to split sufficient for a week or so's supply of kindling.

The First floor
The stairs to the first floor were a continuation of the narrow hall. Two steps from the top and straight ahead was Father's 'office'. The last two treads wound to the left, enabling one to reach the landing leading to the front bedrooms. There were four rooms on this floor, with communication doors allowing one to pass from one room to another so as to arrive back at the stairs without retracing one's steps, an arrangement of which we made full use as children, in our play and in the devising of games. The office, which was immediately above the long narrow scullery, was of similar dimensions.

Although it contained a knee-hole desk and wall shelves crammed with bundles of papers and technical books, I have no memories of my father at work there. I do remember it as a playroom, and can still see in a recess at the far end the large dolls' house, with furniture to scale, made by Father for my sister. I can also remember sleeping there on a camp bed, which fitted under the shelves and allowed just enough space for one to reach the fireplace at the end of the room. No doubt there were occasions when my own room was commandeered for visitors.

The front bedroom was the largest room in the house, longer than the front room below. It was spartan, furnished with only the bare essentials, as the adjoining room, one step down through a curtained archway, was used as a dressing-room. A brass-knobbed bedstead, a massive mahogany bow-fronted chest of drawers and a marble-topped wash-stand, complete with basin, jug and pot, were the main articles of furniture. Two cane-seated chairs and a tripod table completed the furnishings of this, my parents'' room. There was a minute cast iron fireplace in the wall between the bedroom and the dressing-room. I think this wall was once an outer one and only became an internal partition when the side passageway was roofed over to increase the number of bedrooms and attics. A fire was only lit on rare occasions in winter or when illness or convalescence required the sick members of the family to be kept warm and cosy.

The back yard of the house

3

MY FATHER AND GRANDFATHER

'SIR, I HAM A VERY BAD HAND AT RIGHTING.'

I have no record of where my grandfather went to school in Lewes. It was most likely the old British School in Lancaster Street, which was close to York Street where he was born on September 29th 1849. The family lived there until 1877, when they moved to No. 17 North Street nearby. My father attended this school until the spring of 1891, when at the age of fourteen years he was sent as a boarder to Ardingly College. I have a testimonial from James Larwell, the master of the British School, stating that my father had been a scholar there for several years, had passed all the exams of the school with credit and had, here I quote, 'given every satisfaction by his diligence, obedience, and uniformly courteous behaviour'.

How long he was at Ardingly I do not know, most likely until 1895 when he would have been eighteen. In 1896 he was awarded a prize for obtaining a second class in advanced building construction at the annual Examination held at the Lewes School of Science and Art. I still have his prize, a book on Gothic and Renaissance architecture, and also the drawings he submitted for the exam.

No doubt my father was a student at the Lewes School of Art during his apprenticeship to my grandfather. I have no written record of this, but I do have my grandfather's indenture. This parchment, cut so that the irregular edge fitted the half retained by the Master, states that 'William Wells, with the consent of his Father, Thomas Wells, doth put himself apprentice to Henry Card, Builder'. From 1st August 1863, Henry Card was to 'learn his apprentice in the Art of a Carpenter and Joiner' and his 'working hours shall be ten per day', 'all extra hours to be paid for at a rate hereinafter mentioned . . . Three shillings per week for the 1st year, four for the 2nd, five the 3rd, seven the 4th, nine the 5th, and twelve for the 6th and last year.' The document is sealed and signed by my great-grandfather, Thomas Wells, my grandfather, William Wells, and Henry Card, builder, of North Street, Lewes.

It is a strange coincidence that in 1935, while gaining teaching experience in order to sit for the City and Guilds of London Institute Handicraft Examination in relation to woodwork, I spent six months in the old British School, which had been converted into a practical centre for the schools of the town. In the very room where my father had received instruction in the eighteen eighties and, I feel certain, my grandfather also in the eighteen fifties and early sixties, I was giving instruction.

4

MY SCHOOLDAYS

My first school was a private one, run by a Mrs Kenward in a house in Station Street next to an old tobacco shop on the corner. The house is no longer a school, and the shop no longer dispenses tobacco. Although the façades are as they were sixty years ago, the interiors have been altered to suit modern business. I do not know the exact date I started, but it was before the outbreak of war in 1914, most probably in the spring of that year, as I was five years old on the 12th January. My sister was already a pupil, and I can vividly remember going with her on that first morning. A new satchel of canvas and leather, smelling strongly of dressing, slung from my shoulder, held a treasured pencil-box and a piece of Mother's gingerbread for my mid-morning lunch. I remember nothing of lessons as such, but I do remember sitting on Mrs Kenward's lap listening to her telling a story. I also remember using a slate pencil and the scratching noise it made on the slate.

But one memory shines out clear, that is of a game we played in the bay-windowed classroom on the first floor, overlooking the High Street. It was called Family Coach. Mrs Kenward told the story of its journey and spun a plate in the centre of the circle of players. We, the passengers, when mentioned by name, dashed to the plate to keep it spinning, and when the words Family Coach were spoken we all changed places. I never remember the plate breaking on falling, which it frequently did, or being broken by our clumsy efforts to keep it spinning. 1 have no other memories of this school, or when or why my sister and I left.

In the early days of the war, I was a pupil at the Pells Infants School. Here again I have no recollection of lessons but I have one vivid memory of an incident which has left an indelible impression. Nearby was a recreation ground where, before school, we lingered until the last moment, and after school we raced to be the first to reach this adventure playground. This particular afternoon, the patch of sky above the tree-ringed swings was suddenly obscured by an airship flying low over the town. It seemed no more than tree height, but was no doubt higher. That afternoon, with coloured chalks, I sketched on the classroom wallboard my impression of the event. The drawing must have been above average for an infant, for I remember the staff being called to view it and my parents invited to come to see it. For a long time it remained on display, and many were the visitors who commented on my artistic effort. What was so special about the drawing I never knew, but I never produced another work of art that created so much interest.

In the summer of 1916 I was promoted to the Pells National Boys School. I remember little of the teachers in the Infants, but no doubt they gave me a thorough grounding in the three Rs, for my position in class at the end of the first term in Standard 1 of my new school was second. In this class of thirty-one boys, I gained 1,008 marks out of a possible 1,400 for the term, and thirty-four out of forty in the examination. I have in my possession fourteen of my reports, giving term and exam marks, position and number in class, times absent or late, and conduct. No bigger than a postcard, signed by the teacher and dated, they recall many memories of my school days. Without their prompting, many incidents of those formative years would have been forgotten.

Mr E.J. Brooke was the kindly but strict headmaster. The whole of his staff in 1916 were women, the men being away at the war. I remember Mr Cull, during one of his leaves, talking to us of his experiences with the army in France, and a Mr Hudson, in naval uniform, telling us of the war at sea. Mr Cull returned and was my form-master in 1919, but I have no memory of seeing Mr Hudson again.

A Mrs Everett was my teacher for my first term in Standard 1. The next term, the first of a new school year, this became Class VII and Mrs Cull was its mistress. By mid-summer 1920 and by rapid and regular promotions I had reached Class 1B. The following year I was second in Class IA and in 1922, at the age of thirteen, was third in Class 1, which was the headmaster's class. In that year I sat an examination for a place at the Old Grammar School, but was not successful. I therefore ended my school days with another year in Class 1, and had the satisfaction of finishing top.

Great attention was always paid to the three Rs in all the schools I attended. No one left at fourteen unable to read, write or count. We learned arithmetic by writing out and chanting tables, and we could add, subtract and divide with speed. We could not be overcharged in the sweet shop, for we knew to a farthing how much everything ought to cost. We learned by rote facts and figures, dates and data. Knowledge by this method was imprinted on the brain in indelible letters.

Unfamiliar words we were encouraged to look up in the dictionary. We therefore had to know how to spell. We kept lists of unusual words. I still have one of my notebooks with pages of words and their meanings. It is full of other facts and figures, columns of countries and capitals, rivers and mountains, lists of kings and queens, wars and battles, treaties and important events, all with their dates. It is a mine of information. Dog-eared now, the well thumbed pages are evidence of much use by its owner fifty years ago. We learned the difference between 'their' the pronoun and 'there' the adverb, and that 'i' came before 'e' except after 'c'. The rhythm of the rhyme implanted the fact in the young mind.

Similarly, the verse composed long ago by an anonymous author helped us to remember the lengths of the months, and who is likely to forget the discovery of America after chanting, 'Columbus sailed the ocean blue, in fourteen hundred and ninety-two'? It is easier to remember facts as rhymes or verse. Maths tables chanted rhythmically stick in the mind: learnt this way they are 'memorable'. Today this method is considered wrong, but I know what nine sevens or twelve sixes are, as readily as my own name.

In the Infants we had used slates and slate pencils, or boards and chalk. These allowed us a second chance, as mistakes could be rubbed out and corrected. We now used pens and ink, which demanded concentration and no errors. Modern children know nothing of inkwells clogged with dust and paper, and the hazard of an obscene blot as one dipped pen into ink. Or of the messy weapon used by boys, the pellet of blotting-paper, dipped in ink and flicked at an enemy.

My last four years of schooling were spent in the same schoolroom. Three classes were crowded into that long narrow space. Curtains on rods separating the desks of Standards V, VI and VII were no protection from the pin or pen prodded surreptitiously, nor sufficiently soundproof to prevent a whispered conversation between inattentive schoolboys. The headmaster had charge of the two top groups, and Standard V was in the care of the senior master. Their desks were either side of an open fire, which roasted everyone in its vicinity but left the far ends of that elongated room bitterly cold. Two smaller classrooms, either side of the main building, were heated by combustion stoves. On the rear red-hot tops of these, during the absence of the teacher, we would spit, in order to watch the spittle bubble and evaporate. Although at times the cast iron glowed, the heat did not reach the corners of these small rooms.

We were expected to be obedient and we respected the authority of the teacher by being silent in class. The discipline of the Victorian and Edwardian eras spilled over to my generation, and I am glad of it.

5

SUNDAY SCHOOL
AND CHOIR

From an early age I attended Sunday School as an infant, in a class held each Sunday afternoon in the parish room. Then, as a junior and later as a senior, I received instruction for an hour each Sunday before marching in procession to the church for the first part of the morning service. During the singing of the hymn before the sermon we were led out of the galleries and dismissed, but in the afternoon we were back at church for our own service, this time occupying and filling the nave.

I did not sit with my class, for as soon as I was able to read well enough I joined the church choir. I was no more than six or seven when I was accepted as a probationer, for I have clear recollections of the Wednesday evening services, during which the names of casualties of the First World War were read out, and I vividly remember the lists of the wounded, the missing and the killed, lengthening each week. They were names of men I knew, friends of our family, and some fathers of my companions.

I was fortunate to join the choir during its heyday, and in having a thorough training from a choir mistress experienced in church music and voice production. Each day from twelve until one, after singing scales and voice training exercises, we ran through the psalms and canticles, hymns and anthems, for the Sunday services.

Two evenings a week we practised with the tenors and basses and on Saturday attended a special practice for soloists. A great deal of time was given to the choir and its activities, for not only did we sing the church services but we also gave concerts of operatic choruses, duets and songs in the town and parish halls. Rehearsals for these were held after the regular choir practice, or on another evening.

The average length of a boy's service with the choir was four to five years before adolescence changed his pure treble into a cracked travesty of a voice. The majority left when this happened. A few continued as altos until the voice developed into the high tenor or the lower baritone of the adult male. I remained a member of the choir for over twenty years, graduating from childish treble to baritone. I sang the services of the church, the solos and soprano parts of duets, trios and quartets in anthems and oratorios, until the occasion when, following the tenor who in the Hymn of Praise had just sung, 'Watchman, what of the night?', my voice cracked on the high note of the soprano's short reply, 'The night is departing, depar –'.

After that embarrassment I sang in a lower register, pieces more suited to my changing voice. I had joined the choir when there was competition for a place, but with the departure of the organist and the arrival of a new rector change was inevitable. Our numbers declined and, unable through lack of members to perform a whole work, we sang excerpts. We gave no more recitals or concerts. Parishioners no longer filled the church or the public the halls. Live music was being replaced by recorded. The choruses and songs, anthems and oratorios, the great music of the church, indeed the services themselves, at the throw of a switch, could now be heard in the comfort of the home.

Sunday School treats

The Sunday School treats were red letter days in my childhood. Momentous occasions, impatiently awaited, animatedly enjoyed and savoured long after. Maybe it was because I was of an age full of awe and curiosity, vigour and vitality, and that those outings and entertainments were my first experience of organised excursions. I never remember the day of the treat as other than hot and blazing. The skies seemed always blue and cloudless, whether the outings were to the meadows or to the sea.

We assembled at the parish room after an early and hurried dinner, formed up and marched with our teachers to a meadow at Brown's Farm at Landport, a distance of well over a mile but a short step to excited youngsters. On arrival at the field we were handed over to officials who organised races and games. We scrambled for handfuls of sweets, and played cricket. Egg and spoon, three-legged and sack races kept us occupied until a substantial tea, set out on long trestle tables under the trees, subdued our excitement and brought a memorable day to a close. I have no memory of how we returned, whether we marched in an orderly column or shuffled home in straggling groups, but return we did, no doubt tired and weary from the excitements and exertions of the day.

The outings to the seaside were organised and carried out with similar military precision, assembling at the church hall, forming up and marching off in classes through the town to the railway station. There was very little traffic to impede our progress, and no waiting for the train, for reserved coaches stood in a siding awaiting our arrival and the coupling of the steam engine, an engine that seemed as excited as the children to get to the sea as quickly as possible. Our destination was usually Seaford, a distance of nine or ten miles. A journey over all too soon for some, for many had not often travelled by train, but for most it was a procrastination of anticipated thrills and bliss.

Scrambling out of the train, we were quickly formed into an orderly crocodile and marched to the hall, where later we would return ravenously hungry, to devour the bread and butter, buns and cakes, and slake our thirst with lemonade and tea prepared for us by a willing band of helpers who had arrived with laden hampers by an earlier train. Here we were divided into manageable groups and, accompanied by an adult, we hurried through the town and along the grassy causeway over the saltings to the groyned beach.

No one bathed but most, except the timorous, paddled, shrieking at the sudden shock of the surf on unaccustomed feet. Boys threw stones tirelessly at the uncomplaining sea, skated flat ones across its surface, set up targets on the groyne and from the limitless supply selected ammunitions to knock them down again. The girls had their own ways of enjoying the sun and sea during the all too short afternoon. Some encouraged the boys to feats of daring on the wooden groynes, or to balance precariously on a pile, but most sat and giggled, or strolled arm in arm along the beach until the shrill blast of a whistle gathered the scattered groups for a reluctant return to the hall. The jam tarts and iced buns, gingerbread and plum cake, quickly alleviated our unwillingness to leave the beach, and when we regretfully had to refuse another tart we were ready to walk wearily to the station and board the train that would take us to home and bed.

6

EARLY MEMORIES

The aeroplane

I was no more than two years old when I saw my first aeroplane. I have not been able to confirm the date, but I am certain that it was sometime in 1911 when this momentous event occurred to leave an indelible impression on my young mind. In that year there was a race around Britain, and I believe the plane I saw was a competitor. The machine was flying towards Brighton following the valley between Kingston and the Race Hill, where a large crowd had gathered to watch its progress. It was certainly expected, as people had assembled some time before its arrival. The memory of that moment, of the man and machine moving across the sky not far above my head, has remained with me all my life.

My mother, accompanied by an aunt, wheeled me in my push-chair to Spital Barn on the summit of the hill. From this elevated position above the town one has extensive views of the county. To the north-east one can see the green and gold tapestry of the Weald as far as the forest ridge. To the east, the red roofs and weathered stone of the town and the white chalk of the Cliffe hills. Beyond them Caburn, and the whole undulating line of Downs from Firle to the Cuckmere and the distant massive group which terminates at Beachy Head. To the south one can follow the meanderings of the Ouse through the broad valley between Itford and Kingston and glimpse the grey-green sea seven miles away, while to the west and north the swelling Downs roll away to the horizon and beyond. These hills became a school and a playground, and the panoramas from their summits are colour-printed in my memory.

I was too young on that day to notice or appreciate the view, but I clearly remember the excitement of the crowd when the plane appeared south of the town, and of my attention being drawn to the skeletal machine of canvas and wire trundling across the sky just above my head and being told there was a man in it. This historic event, for few on that concourse had seen a flying machine until that day, was recalled many times in after years, and maybe the retelling has kept the memory of that astonishing sight from fading. Thirty years later I thought of that day when, as an officer in the Royal Air Force, I met many of the pilots who at greater heights, and in faster and more sophisticated machines, fought and won the Battle of Britain above those hills.

In August 1940 there was a remarkable sequel•. The aunt who was with my mother on that day in 1911 was walking with a friend on that same hilltop when, from the south, a German biplane flying low and following the river valley circled the hill and landed close by. The pilot, unhurt, climbed out and with hands raised walked towards them, but members of the Home Guard and Observer Corps arrived and he surrendered to them. It was afterwards reported that the plane was carrying mail for the occupation troops in the Channel Islands, and that the pilot had lost his way in a sea fog.

The railway

My earliest remembered journeys by train were ones to the seaside. These were necessarily short as we lived no more than seven miles from the coast. Our destination was usually Seaford or Bishopstone, for a picnic on the beach, or to Brighton for more sophisticated amusement. I associate the latter resort and its entertainments with those excursions when Father accompanied us and the former with those organised by Mother. These outings occurred frequently throughout the summer months and the journeys were therefore during daylight hours.

I do not remember travelling in a train after dark until I was much older, but I do remember the unlit train entering the darkness of the short tunnel at Falmer, passing through and emerging into the sunlight at its Brighton

---

•*See also* Lewes at War 1939-1945, *by R.A.Elliston, S.B.Publications, 1999.*

end. Stations and platforms in those days were lit by hissing gas jets, and the signal lamps by oil, the porters having to climb the iron gantry ladders to light them. At the smaller stations and halts the gas lamps were turned down when no train was expected, and up again when one was due. I have seen this dimming at country stations and even in the booking hall at Lewes, but not on the platforms there. No doubt the frequency of the trains and the length of the many platforms prevented the practice at this busy junction. With electrification the plopping gas and smoky oil lamps disappeared. Another casualty of this era was the wheeltapper who, on the arrival of the train, leapt from the platform to the track and with a long-handled hammer struck each wheel, I'm sure not stopping long enough to hear if they were cracked. No doubt he still performed this labour, but in some remote unelectrified siding, screened from the fascinated eyes of envious boys.

The trains were made up of First, Second and Third class carriages, luggage and guards' vans. Who travelled in the Second class carriages and in what way they differed from the other two, I do not know. We usually travelled Third, only in the First class if the train was crowded. In those days one asked the guard to unlock a compartment and paid him the extra to travel in greater comfort, six to a carriage instead of ten, seated on deep-cushioned anti-macassared seats with adjustable arms, with one's feet on a carpeted floor.

The upholstered benches of the Third class were less sumptuous and above their harder padded backs, instead of panelled mirrors, were framed advertisements and coloured views of southern beauty spots. Placed between the adverts for Colman's Mustard and Beechams Pills, a lever on a graduated scale allowed the passengers to control and regulate the steam heater on the lino-covered floor beneath the seats, but we were more interested in the panorama rushing by, of the woods and fields, the streams and hills, than in photographs of the countryside or advertisements of condiments and pills.

A number of times I travelled in the luggage van. This one was allowed to do when no seats were available, and each compartment had its complement of standing passengers. In the windowless wooden box, once the doors were closed, one travelled in semi-darkness, seated on packing-cases and sacks of merchandise. We children revelled in such a romantic conveyance, but our parents did not share our enchantment. On one memorable day we travelled to Brighton in a saloon carriage. These were double the size of a normal compartment, most comfortable and beautifully furnished. Easy chairs flanking a central table, a sofa fixed to one wall and seats to the other, accommodated eight to ten people. A small mahogany-panelled cloakroom, fitted with wash-hand-basin and toilet, completed the suite.

What a splendid sight it was, to sit on a hillside in that age of steam and watch a plume of smoke threading its way through the countryside. To follow the progress of an invisible train speeding across the Weald until with hurrying whistle, faint at first then rising to a crescendo, it bursts from a cutting into view, rushing over crossing, bridge and causeway, impatient to reach the coast. No more are seen such stirring sights, no more does one hear the jingle and rattle of milk cans being loaded onto or out of vans. We took it all for granted and did not foresee the time would come when it would end.

The seaside

I remember nothing of my first visit to the seaside, but I do know the date. I have in my possession a picture postcard of Cuckmere Haven, sent by my mother to my aunt. It was posted in Seaford and is dated 20th July 1909. Mother's message reads, 'We are here for the day. Alice is frightened of the sea, but Baby quite enjoys it.' Alice, my sister, was then three years old and I a mere six months, much too young to remember the occasion.

My earliest distinct memory of the sea is of a ride on Volk's Railway from Brighton Palace Pier to Black Rock. I vividly remember the portion of the track that was built on trestles so that at high tide one had the impression of travelling on the sea. I'm sure this experience implanted the trip in my young mind. I never again remember the sea so close, and began to believe it had not happened, until quite recently I read that this used to be so, before wind and tide piled up the shingle around and under the trestled track, so that the sea no longer lapped the line.

This incident was most certainly before the First World War, and I remember that Father was with me on this occasion. Usually it was Mother who took us to the seaside, accompanied by one or more of her friends and their children who were our age. Most of our excursions were day trips to the beach at Bishopstone. In those days the old London Brighton and South Coast Railway still halted an occasional train at the exposed wooden platform built in Victorian times to serve the isolated cottages and tide mills. The village of Bishopstone was a mile distant in a hollow of the Downs. The mills were once a thriving community, but had long since fallen into disuse, and most of the buildings were empty. It was but a short walk past the ruined sluices and races of the mill, and the boarded-up doors and windows of the now unoccupied cottages, to the pebbled beach where seakale, struggling to survive, was the only vegetation on that shingle bank which edged the curve of the bay. At low tide there was an expanse of sand created by the combined curves of breakwater and bay. In the summer heat it shimmered, and the sea like a blue bale of shiny silk unrolled itself, fold upon fold upon its rippled surface. An untidy line of flotsam, weed and wood, drying in the sun and wind, marked the limit of the highest tide, and dead starfish and sundry shells awaited the next to carry them back to sea again, a blue-green sea whose foaming edge formed a lacy hem to the beach.

I cannot remember how one paid one's fare or obtained a ticket, as there was no porter or even a signal-box at the halt. On the landward side there was a gate across the stony road to prevent cattle wandering on to the line, but on the seaward side there was nothing between the embankment and the shingle. The whole of the foreshore was railway property and I remember, during the war, long lines of trucks in the sidings full of guns, shells and war equipment awaiting shipment to France.

There were no mobile snack bars to relieve Mother of the chore of picnic preparation, or ice-cream vans to cheer the children. If insufficient food and drink was brought from home, one either went without or faced a long walk to the few shops around the harbour, a mile or more away. We had no thermos flasks. Water brought with us was heated on a methylated spirit stove for the making of tea to revive the grown-ups, and tepid lemonade, sipped throughout the day, refreshed the hot and thirsty youngsters.

An event which always created a commotion in the bay and on the beach was the arrival of the afternoon cross-Channel boat. Its coming was eagerly awaited with mounting excitement, but with a certain amount of regret, as it heralded the beginning of the end of our day's outing. We would vie with each other to be the first to see the speck of smoke in the haze where the sky and the blue sea merged. We watched the dot grow larger as the boat drew near. If the tide was out, we strengthened the defences of the castles we had built on the exposed strip of sand, in the hope they would withstand the bow wave of the approaching steamer. They never did, and when the breakers had subsided the sand had been swept and smoothed, and none of our fortifications remained. At high tide the sudden surge of the sea drove the family groups further up the beach, and the hasty gathering together of picnic paraphernalia was the beginning of the preparation for our departure.

7

A MISCELLANY OF MEMORIES

Aprons

My mother's parents lived in a terraced cottage toward the western end of the road which runs through the centre of Lewes. From the low ground to the east, this road crosses the river on an ancient stone bridge of a single massive arch, before climbing the steep hill, bordered by graceful Georgian houses, to reach the upper part of the High Street. Here, with the castle keep upon its mote as a dramatic backcloth, tile-hung timber-framed houses and shops line its length. It then ascends a gentler slope between stone and flint faced buildings of great charm, narrows and levels off among rows of uniform Victorian cottages, whose front doors open onto red brick pavements. Here, where the road forks, the left arm following the valley to Brighton, the right hugging the contours of the hills to the villages of the Weald, was the 'two up and two down' home of my grandparents.

My grandmother died when I was quite young, but I have clear memories of her in a black, high-necked, severe Edwardian dress, the skirt of which was always protected by a freshly laundered snow-white apron. In my childhood it was a common sight to see men and women about the town in aprons. Housewives popped out to the corner shop wearing the coarse apron of the kitchen, or the housemaid on an errand, in one of white linen with bib and frills. Tradesmen too had their distinctive aprons. The butchers and fishmongers wore ones of blue and white striped material, while those of the brewery workers – there were seven breweries in the town – were tailored from hessian hop pockets.[*]

---

[*] *Moleskin aprons were usually provided by breweries for their workmen.*

Blacksmiths and farriers – it was said there were more racing stables than places of worship, seven churches and many chapels – favoured leather for its hard-wearing qualities and its ability to withstand the heat and sparks from the glowing metal when practising their craft. Male domestics, and those employed by the numerous hotels and inns as boots or potmen, found green baize an ideal material. Bakers, grocers and shop-keepers in general all wore aprons of white, tied at the waist with tapes, the bib being held up by a tape loop round the neck or buttoned to the wearer's waistcoat. The most common apron to be seen was the white twill of the carpenters, but not all who wore them were workers in wood. Before the advent of the overall, this type of apron was the universal protective garment and was worn by men in the home when carrying out their house-hold chores. I myself wore one from a very early age. At first its purpose was to keep my clothes clean, but later to protect them when I was performing my many daily and weekly tasks. When I was apprenticed, I wore my carpenter's apron with pride, taking care not to soil it unnecessarily, for in our workshop a dirty apron indicated a slovenly workman, and slovenly men and work were not tolerated.

I have memories of many an aproned character, who because of his or her 'uniform' I remember today. There was the 'Trotter Man' who, in a spotless one of white, stood in the High Street each Saturday night purveying cooked pigs' trotters from a wicker basket covered with a snow-white cloth. I believe his name was Short. His brother worked at Pryor's pork shop in the High Street, from where no doubt he obtained his wares. At the railway station a pinafored old lady sold buttonholes to the travellers. In all winds and weathers she was to be seen with her basket of seasonal posies, carnations and roses for the lapels of her regular customers. Before breakfast, the white-aproned 'hot roll man' summoned us to the door with his bell, and in the afternoon the muffin-man, similarly attired, tempted us with his confections.

Another character was an old lady whom one sent for to 'lay out' the deceased. I never remember seeing her about the town on business without a starched white apron over her ankle-length black dress.

This leads me back to the reason for recording recollections of these garments. The tale has been told and retold, by Mother and her sisters, of the occasion when royalty acknowledged the smile and wave of my grandmother. Lewes in those days possessed a race course, and followers of the sport arrived in the town by train. They either walked the hilly two miles to the course or rode in one of the many horse-drawn vehicles that plied for hire and crowded the streets on race days. All race-goers, whether on foot or travelling by carriage, had to traverse the High Street, and in so doing passed the home of my grandparents. On such days my grandmother would watch the animated scene from behind the lace curtains of the front room, but on this occasion she watched the hurrying crowd from the front doorstep. Maybe she had previous knowledge and was waiting in anticipation – my grandfather had connections with the racing fraternity and had perhaps received inside information – but happen it did, and the incident has been told and retold thus. In an open carriage among the stream of horse-drawn vehicles taking the flinty road to the race course was King Edward VII. My grandmother, in her usual black dress and starched white apron, smiled and waved. The King turned his head toward her, smiled and waved his hand in acknowledgment. Was it her smile or her apron that caught the royal eye? I like to think it was the latter, and that humble snow-white garment received His Majesty's approval.

Pocket money

As a child I was never given a regular amount of pocket money. What little I did receive I was encouraged to save and most of it went immediately into my money-box. I owned many money-boxes, but not all at the same time. The majority were so designed that coins could be easily inserted, but there was no way to extract them when the need arose other than by using force, thereby rendering the box unfit for further use. Many were made of tinplate and the opening was easily damaged by the kitchen knife we used when endeavouring to remove a few coppers surreptitiously. From time to time a sixpence or a shilling was given to me by an uncle or an aunt – on my birthday it could be as much as half a crown – but these occasions were rare, and the silver would be quickly be posted in a miniature pillarbox, which in my childhood was a popular form of money-box. I can't remember for what I saved, most probably it was for additions to my clockwork trains or Meccano set, or for gifts to the family at Christmas and eggs at Easter.

There was no shortage of sweets at home, so we were not often tempted to spend our coppers on the confections of the corner shop. Dishes on sideboard and chiffonier were never empty of boiled sweets or toffees, but chocolates were a rarity. These were kept in a cupboard and only produced on special occasions. We were not allowed to help ourselves to sweets, only taking one when given permission to do so. Often we were refused, it being either too near a meal or that we had had more than was good for us. When we did spend our pennies, what a selection the shop had to offer. For a farthing we had the choice of many sugary delights. Liquorice laces and sherbet dabs, aniseed balls or acid drops, and a great variety of brightly coloured boiled sweets from the bottles and boxes on counter and shelf. A penny would buy almost anything displayed in the shop and window. We bought chocolate novelties at Christmas and eggs at Easter, but at other times of the year our pennies would be spent on quantity rather than quality: long-lasting toffees and 'gob-stoppers' rather than the softer sweets which we considered poor value for our money. The one exception was perhaps sherbet, for we loved the taste of the fizzy foam upon the tongue.

We had a number of sources of income. One was the rag and bone merchant. Rabbit was frequently on our menu, and for our 'help' in its preparation for the pot we would claim the skin, for which we could be sure of at least a penny. Another source was an old couple who lived nearby and kept chickens on an allotment the husband had created on a portion of the castle wall. He was a jobbing builder and had adapted his ruin to form terraces, no more than a few feet wide, on which he grew vegetables and kept his livestock. The levels were reached by very steep steps, up which no doubt the soil for this miniature smallholding was carried by its creator. He was arthritic and used his bicycle for support for his crippled body, and a bucket in which he transported the scraps for his hens from his home to his plot. For vegetable peelings and other food scraps we collected, we could always be sure of a farthing from the old lady. This source of income dried up when Father decided to keep chickens and arrived home with a dozen pullets. From that moment we collected food for our hens and no doubt benefited more from their eggs than from the sweets we would have bought with the farthing.

When I was a boy, a farthing was a fortune, not only to children, but to many families whose weekly budget was a pennyworth of this and a pennyworth of that. But what a lot could be purchased with a penny. Herrings at twenty-four a shilling, hot rolls two a penny, sugar, rice and flour weighed and bagged while you waited, all for coppers. Eggs at sixpence a dozen, and oranges at Christmas at a halfpenny. I thought of those days when looking through my boyhood stamp collection. One can see how the currency has depreciated by looking at the lowest value of present-day Christmas stamps. When I was a boy we could post four hundred and eighty Christmas cards for one pound; today we can post only fourteen.[*]

Toys, games and pastimes
The toys and games of my childhood were simple and unsophisticated and there is no comparison between them and the detailed working scale models or the mass-produced moulded plastic toys of today. We derived much joy and satisfaction from making our own playthings, using scrap material from work basket and workshop, but at Christmas or on birthdays we were happy to receive toys of a more lasting nature. Wooden ones soundly constructed and gaily painted were appreciated, and tinplate toys with simple clockwork mechanisms that amazed or amused were treasured and prized. A key was needed to wind the clockwork of the model trains, mechanical men or animals. If you lost it, it was not too difficult to find another as the whole toy world was run on clockwork in those days. If the electronic circuitry of today's sophisticated toys breaks down, it needs more than a few ratchety turns of a key to get it going again. Each toy or game was carefully replaced in its box, and all were packed away in the wooden toy

[*] *Mr Wells was writing when 2nd class stamps were 7p!*

chest after play. I still have this chest, but none of the toys except a number of lead soldiers. Some are on horseback, others on foot, as brightly coloured in their varied uniforms today as they were on their first parade, but alas many are now without arm or leg, lost in battles fought long ago.

From wood and cloth, sticks and string, we made and shaped simple playthings. We hollowed the young elder stems for pea shooters and popguns, removing the soft spongy pith with pocket knife, nail or needle, and using hips, haws and green elderberries for ammunition, only resorting to dried peas when the berries were not in season. We hollowed shoots for whistle pipes, sometimes succeeding in producing a pleasing tone, but more often than not the result was a scale of discordant notes. The straight growths of the hedgerow hazel we cut and fashioned for many of our games, weapons and pastimes. From short lengths we shaped handles for the whips for our tops, or for the stock-whips with which we tried to emulate the cowboys of the Wild West shows that periodically visited the town. A wire nail driven in one end of a whittled stick, and carefully bent with pliers, was a skid for our iron hoops, made for us by the local blacksmith. From longer and thicker lengths we made bows, using waxed cobbler's thread for the string. For arrows we preferred garden canes, but if unable to acquire them we chose the straightest of the thinner hazel shoots. We achieved a reasonable distance with these weapons, but their accuracy left much to be desired.

We fished in the river, brooks and ponds, with home-made rods of cane or hazel. To our lines of thread we attached the largest hook from our collection, the supposition being, the larger the hook the larger the fish we would catch, but we were never still long enough to entice the wary creatures to within catching distance. We were always moving noisily to what we thought was a better spot if, after a few minutes casting, our efforts had not met with success. Before aspiring to a rod, we caught sticklebacks and tadpoles with a net, usually a bought one, as the mesh of lace curtains which we used for our primitive efforts was too large to trap these tiny creatures. These nets were dual purpose. When not used for pond dipping we chased butterflies with them, through the meadows and over the Downs, with not much more success than our efforts to catch the darting fish. The minnows we did catch never survived for long in their jam-pot, but sometimes the tadpoles lived to develop legs. More often than not we returned our catches to the ponds and brooks, or somehow, somewhere managed to lose them before we reached home.

Other games also come to my mind, those we played and improvised during the long winter evenings when the early fall of darkness shortened the day and curtailed our outdoor activities. As soon as tea was over and the table had been cleared of the remains, the white cloth was removed and over the bobble-trimmed Paisley fabric beneath was spread a protective covering of paper if paints or crayons, pastes or glues were to be used to colour or decorate scrapbooks. or to assemble cardboard cut-out toys. If games with cards, dice or dominoes, however, were to occupy the all too short time between tea and bed, then the pile of this carpet of a table-cloth was an ideal playing surface.

This magnificent table covering was much too heavy to be shaken like any normal cloth to rid it of crumbs which had found their way through lacy table-cloths. A crumb brush could not always reach the debris deep within its pile. Only by beating while hanging on a line would the most obstinate scraps and particles be dislodged. It received and survived this regular pummelling until the war, when it fell victim to the bomb which wrecked our home and damaged the table it had so long clothed and graced.

From an early age I had been taught and had played a variety of card games, no doubt encouraged to do so to exercise my mental faculties and to stimulate an interest in numbers. Of them all, cribbage was the one I most enjoyed. For many years I played an evening hand with Mother, until the permutations and the scoring combinations of the cards were automatic. Dominoes was another game that trained my mind to memorise and calculate the consequence of playing the pieces. I played both games regularly with Mother, and when older was allowed to visit my grandfather for a nightly hand of 'cribb' or dominoes. I graduated to these more adult games under their influence and guidance, but played Snap, Beat Your Neighbour Out of Doors and other boisterous card games of our own devising with my sister and friends.

The names of many of the games played with counters, moved on a board to the throw of a dice, are forgotten. Interest in these faded when superseded by newer and more novel games and they, in their turn, would be discarded for a fresh version of an old amusement. But the old favourites, Snakes and Ladders and Ludo, never lost their appeal. These sedentary games were complemented by versions of the more active party ones which we adapted to suit the restricted conditions of our living-room. We hunted a thimble instead of a slipper or parcel. We raced cut-out shapes of tissue paper, usually frogs or beetles, by blowing them across the table top instead of fanning with cardboard across the floor, but the first past the post received no prize as was usual at a party.

Games that tested the memory were always popular, often played while sitting in the twilight of a summer's evening or in the firelight on a winter's night. A favourite was one where the first player named an article in his 'Grandmother's basket'. The second player named this and added another, and so on, the game continuing with each player repeating all the articles in the right sequence and adding another. A player dropped out of the game if an object was omitted or the list was recited in the wrong order, the winner being the player with the most retentive memory.

Fears, phantasies and phantoms

I have no memory of being afraid of the dark in those candle and lamp-lit days of early childhood. I was never nervous of going up the dim stairs, to the unlit bedrooms and attics, before the installation of electric lights dispelled the shadows and lit the many nooks and crannies of those upper rooms, but tales of ghosts and the supernatural I did not entirely dismiss as fairy stories, and bogymen, sometimes used by Mother to scare us into good behaviour, I half believed in.

From an early age I had 'helped' my aunt in her duties as parish clerk and general factotum of St John's. I had no qualms at being alone in the dim church after an evening service, straightening hassocks or collecting hymn books, or of a winter's night ensuring that no one was inside, by walking through the darkened building before locking the porch door. But I must admit on moonless nights I quickened my step through the churchyard on my way to choir practice, never quite sure of the solidity of the marble memorial figures.

My grandfather had been an undertaker, and the workshop still hoarded in odd corners funeral paraphernalia of the Victorian and Edwardian eras. We often raided these boxes of fancy cotton material, using the drapes and coffin linings in our games. It was therefore no shock to me when I saw a corpse for the first time, whose I do not know, laid out in a cotton shift in a coffin padded and frilled with similar material to what we had used in play. It was the custom of the period for the deceased to be on 'display' for any who wished to call and pay their last respects. The whole neighbourhood would mourn and all blinds would be pulled down or curtains drawn across windows facing the street, until after the funeral. Not only those of the departed's home, but also many of the neighbours showed their regard and sorrow in this manner. In those days people were more conversant with the aspects of mortality. The majority died in their own beds and families lived with their dead until the interment.

It was the convention for the mourners to wear deep black and customary to use notepaper and send memorial cards edged in black. I still have a number of these cards, and it is noticeable that the width of the edging steadily decreases from a very wide band in Victorian times until it is non-existent in the nineteen thirties. The mourning carriages and the giant boxlike hearses were drawn by black horses and proceeded at a walking pace. A hush would fall upon the High Street as the cortege progressed along its length. Groups would stop gossiping and men and boys would stand bareheaded until it had passed. A quiet moment of respect for an old inhabitant, or perhaps a stranger, only broken by the sound of the horses' hooves and the iron-rimmed carriage wheels on the gritty surface of the road. On one occasion I was one of four boys of our choir who had the unenviable task of carrying the coffin of one of our colleagues from his home to the church, a distance of over a quarter of a mile, through streets lined with the people he had grown up among, and heading a procession of his sorrowing family and friends. It was a never-to-be-forgotten experience.

The churchyard of St John's is situated on a promontory, and I remember seeing a small skull exposed by an earthslip on its steep northern bank, but further aided and abetted landslides did not reveal any other bones. The ancient burial ground had long ago been filled, and with no possibility of extending its area the older portions had to be reused. We were therefore interested in any new excavations, hoping that the grave-digger would unearth bones of an earlier inhumation. This he frequently did; the larger fragments of the skeletal remains were reinterred but many, smaller and broken, stained and discoloured, were carried away with surplus soil and dumped on a huge accumulation of earth and rubbish deposited by generations of grave-diggers.

I often thought what a sorting out and scrambling for missing parts there would be in that pile and what a turmoil in the churchyard on the day of resurrection. I had a boy's healthy indifference to mortality and tended to agree with Mother, whom I remember once remarking, 'We have more to fear from the living than the dead'.

I was not unduly daunted by tales of bogymen. They were used to intimidate rather than frighten. One such tale I remember was of a character known as Spring-heeled Jack. This story was based on a real person of Victorian times whose escapades terrified Londoners. He sprang upon them from dark alleyways, and relieved them of their valuables. In the versions of the story that were told to us, he was tall and hooded, and had powerful springs fitted to the heels of his shoes which enabled him to leap over hedges or to peer into bedroom windows. I'm not sure of the purpose of this fable but I do remember that we imitated him, without the aid of springs, in trying to scare friends by jumping out at them from doorways.

We were told many tales of ghosts, haunted houses, churchyards and crossroads. We heard about these supernatural happenings from various sources and the stories were told and retold by older boys to the newer and younger members of the choir, club or gang. We knew of the ghostly witch-hounds that could be heard on the Downs at night, and of the spectre of a murderess who moaned on moonless nights and on moonlit ones was to be seen at a certain crossroads. We were told of apparitions that would appear if one ran a certain number of times around a particular spot, but I knew of no one who had sufficient courage to complete the required laps needed for phantoms to emerge from tumulus or tomb. These stories were similar to those possibly started and circulated by the smugglers many years before, with the intention of keeping the hills, lanes and trackways clear of prying eyes. Smugglers had an obvious interest in frightening people away, and no doubt these tales were told to us to ensure that we returned home well before dark.

The circus

The visit of a circus was an event looked forward to with excitement and talked about long afterwards with amazement. My first recollection of one was not of an actual performance but of the parade of circus folk and animals through the town which, weather permitting, always preceded a show, promising even greater marvels when appearing later and performing their acts in the sawdust ring under the canvas roof of their huge portable theatre. I could not have been very old when I first saw that animated pageant, as I vividly remember being in a push-chair. Whether 1 had been taken especially to see the procession or whether we were on our way to visit Grandmother, who lived near the fairground, I do not know, but I can still see that glittering cavalcade, as it gaily advanced down the hill toward my own private grandstand on the raised pavement outside what is now the Shelleys Hotel.

In those pre-1914 years there were many more circuses touring the country during the summer months than there were in the years after the war. Most were small family concerns just making a living, but they brought as much joy with their great talents as their larger brothers did with their speciality acts, sideshows and menageries. There were a number of sites within the town boundaries for the tents, and the numerous wagons necessary for the transport of the equipment and the accommodation of man and beast. The larger circuses pitched their tents on the Race Hill fairground. Here there was ample room for the enormous steam engines, which drew as many as four box wagons of equipment and baggage from town to town and, when uncoupled from their train of vans, generated power by day and night to illuminate the tent, booths and fairground with strings of coloured lights. Here there was also sufficient room for the horse-drawn caravans of the performers and the cages of the animals which, if not part of the act, were exhibited to the public for a few pence, and advertised as the world's largest, smallest, most ferocious or oddest.

The smaller circuses, principally Wild West shows, were sited on waste ground near the old fire station. These were given in a tent pitched on the clinkered surface. No sawdust was spread in the ring, consequently clouds of dust enveloped everyone when the Indians attacked the Deadwood coach as it was driven furiously round the ring before being rescued by a troop of cowboys. There were no clowns in this type of show. The individual acts were demonstrations of skill with ropes, stock whips, knife throwing and target practice with revolvers and rifles. For weeks after such a show we practised lassoing each other and spent many hours endeavouring to get a crack from our improvised stock whips, but with little success. Our interest soon waned and we directed our energies to a newer game or pastime.

The circuses travelled from town to town, and the wagons arrived at the ground at irregular intervals throughout the previous day and night. If the distance was not too great the elephants and camels walked all the way, otherwise a special train conveyed them to the nearest railway siding. The elephants in procession were a sight that delighted every child who saw them. The ponderous creatures swinging along in single file, trunk grasping the tail ahead, were an incongruous sight in the ancient streets, and even more so in a leafy Sussex lane.

The humble circus folk were jacks of all trades. Coming into town at daybreak after travelling all night, they unloaded and erected the tent, groomed the animals and bedecked them for the parade. They took a part in it themselves, dressed in colourful costumes depicting characters of romance and legend, royalty and history, parading the streets on foot or mounted on prancing horses. They were members of the band which usually headed the procession in an ornate gilt horse-drawn wagonette, making up for their lack of numbers by their enthusiastic beating of drums and blowing of trumpets. They perhaps performed at a matinee as well as the evening show, packing everything away at the end of the performance, starting some of the dismantling even before its end. Then off on the road to the next town, whatever the weather, snatching sleep whenever they could.

The clowns never failed to delight. They were loved by all, young and old. They were the very heart of the circus. Comedians of innocuous humour and singers of innocent songs, acrobats, gymnasts and athletes of great ability. Their audience surrounded them so they had to be heard and every gesture and grimace seen. They were the captivating favourites of the children and deserved the applause.

No 12 West Street after the bomb fell in 1940 (see also page 14)

8

FAIRS, MARKETS AND SHOPPING IN LEWES

Sheep fairs

I have a remembrance of looking down upon the street in which we lived, crowded with sheep. Seen from the bedroom window, the jostling, bobbing multitude appeared as a cream carpet moving steadily up the hill. No doubt there were drovers and dogs, but I have no recollection of them nor of bleating, barking or any noise whatever. All I can remember of that moment is that slowly moving mass of sheep.

When I was a boy, sheep, cattle and pigs were driven through the streets to and from the market, but the huge flock below me was probably on its way to the Race Hill where each autumn a Sheep Fair was held. In those days the flocks travelled on foot to the fairground, the majority over the hills from downland farms, but a few from valley farms could not avoid the narrow streets, as they were obliged to cross the river by the old stone bridge in the lower part of the town.

Once over the bridge, the High Street could be bypassed by shepherding the sheep through East Street and West Street, where we lived, and Paddock Road to Race Hill where from time immemorial a fair had been held. Here the whole ground was laid out with a checkerboard pattern of hurdle pens, with passageways between. Arriving at irregular intervals, the flocks caused considerable commotion in the alleyways should two arrive together. Many had been travelling since the grey light of dawn, moving steadily toward the fairground. Some perhaps had started the journey the day before and had stopped overnight at a farm within easy walking distance. Hundreds of sheep were on the move on such days, urged on by the shepherds, their dogs and a host of small boys.

This was also a social occasion for farmers and shepherds, and the voices of man and beast added to the hubbub of that jam-packed fairground. I remember being fascinated by the patter of the auctioneer and could never understand how he knew who was bidding, as no one seemed interested in the pen of sheep he was selling. I also remember the dogs, the shaggy Old English breed which had not yet been ousted by the smoother-coated collie. The most pleasing sound in all the clamour was that of the bells. Whether made from an old can with an iron bolt for a clapper or a work of art forged by the local blacksmith, the range of notes and tones produced was magical. The magic of the Downs was in those bells, the springy turf and the tangy breeze, the brilliant skies and the freedom of those vast smooth hills. I have five of these treasures. Their notes bring back many memories of youthful summers, when the only man-made sound to be heard on the hills was that of the tinkling bells as the flock slowly quartered the turf.

Market days

Monday was the day the town braced itself for the weekly assault on its tranquil way of life. On that day the farming community of the immediate locality, both man and beast, invaded its narrow streets and twittens, and filled its urban air with the sounds and scents of the countryside. It was the day set aside for the flurry and excitement of a cattle market, held in cramped and crowded conditions near the railway station. Although it adjoined the station there was, and still is, no facility for unloading cattle. In my boyhood the panicky steers, sheep and pigs had to be driven through the twisting back streets and alleyways from the goods yard in the Cliffe, where they had arrived from distant parts of Sussex, sometimes during the weekend, to the pens and sale ring of the market-place a mile away. During the holidays we boys were up early on market days. Selecting a stout stick from our varied collection, we hurried to the yard to 'help' the railway staff and drovers unload the wayward beasts, and gently drive and steer them towards their fate. At the end of the day we 'assisted' in driving the lucky ones back to the cattle trucks, to another life, with another farmer, on another farm. The unlucky ones not dealt with in the tiny abattoir in the market were driven by the butchers to their own premises for slaughter. There were a number of these slaughter-houses in the town, and all were sited in narrow streets and passageways. Meeting the terrified animals in these twittens could be a frightening experience. Today many of these buildings are quaint desirable cottages in traffic-free corners of the town, their conversions giving no indication of their previous grisly use, and their present owners, as likely as not, unaware of the butchery that occurred on the site of their now hygienic homes.

The town prepared itself for this weekly invasion of cattle and farming folk. From first light, and before on darker autumn and winter mornings, from the many farms within walking distance, in twos and threes bullocks and heifers, cows and calves, would awaken the sleepy streets with clattering hooves, snortings and much mooing. The drovers' cries and the barking of their dogs, as the small groups converged towards their destiny, added to the hubbub in the narrow approaches and to the apparent chaos of the market.

Hard on the heels of the driven herds came the men and women of the rural economy. In a great variety of horse-drawn vehicles they jangled into town, jamming its labyrinthine lanes and streets with their traps and gigs, farm carts and wagons, unloading agricultural products and human freight from Wealden farms and smallholdings, to the stores and shops of tradesmen. Corn and hay to the chandlers and seedsmen, vegetables and fruit to the greengrocers, and eggs, butter and cheese to the grocers and the dairies of milkmen who, later in the day, would from brass-bound churns on horse-drawn floats or three-wheeled push-carts ladle that morning's milk into the customer's can or jug, and deliver farm-fresh dairy produce.

When the business deals, the bartering and bargaining were completed, these hearty-looking men, loud of voice, corduroy-suited and leather-gaitered, gathered in the bars and tap rooms of the taverns, drinking beer from pint pots and consuming gargantuan lunches in the dining-rooms of the eating houses and pubs. Here one heard the purest Sussex dialect, that broad and sprawling speech of country men, sadly disappearing rapidly. Delightful old-fashioned words and terms, expressive and picturesque, derived from the speech of their Anglo-Saxon ancestors. Hunger and thirst satisfied, wiping with large red handkerchiefs crumbs and froth from whiskered chins on ruddier faces, they noisily went their ways, their hob-nailed boots clattering on the cobbled roads and stone-slabbed pavements.

Sussex was the last bastion of the smock, the only dress this country could claim as a truly national costume. Although it became obsolete during the early years of this century, it persisted as a working article of clothing among the country folk. I remember seeing shepherds at the sheep fairs, and the occasional market drover, wearing this ancient rural garment. Not the white round frock decorated with rich and intricate needlework, worn as Sunday best, but a gabardine made of a tough grey or blue, almost waterproof material, which survived, without needing repair, exposure to the elements and the numerous washes of a lifetime. My Aunt Hilare's father wore such a smock. He was a cobbler and no doubt wore it as a protective garment whilst repairing his customers' footwear. I can see him now, sitting on a stool, surrounded by his cobbling tools and, to the amazement of a very small boy, producing brads in a seemingly unending stream from his mouth and hammering them into the leather sole of a boot on the last laid between his knees.

The grocer's shop

Smells have the ability to evoke memories of people and places. Spice and fruit, cheese and coffee bring to my mind a small grocer's shop where, seated on a bentwood chair, legs dangling clear of the sawdusted floor, I would wait while Mother discussed her order with the white-aproned proprietor. It was one of the few shops I did not mind visiting as a child. The hundred and one scents of the varied stock crammed into the tiny shop mingled to produce a never-to-be-forgotten, tantalising, nose-twitching aroma.

Every inch of floor and wall was used to accommodate the sacks and tubs, bins and canisters containing comestibles. Sacks of dried peas and beans, rice and potatoes, the tops neatly rolled back, were ranged in rows behind the door, and in the corner, raised to allow a jug to be placed under the taps, were a barrel of black treacle and a cask of vinegar. Sides of bacon and bladders of lard hung above huge cheeses and slabs of butter on the marble-topped counter for the dairy produce. Very little of the stock was pre-packed; almost everything had to be weighed and wrapped. I would gaze wide-eyed at cheese being cut into wedges with a wire, bacon sliced by a primitive hand machine, but above all my delight was to watch a shapeless lump of butter moulded into a symmetrical block by a few rapid movements of the wooden butter pats in the grocer's hand.

Dry goods such as tea and sugar, rice or lentils, beans and barley were scooped from bins or poured from canisters into the brass pan of a balance and transferred to a cone-shaped bag which, in a moment of magic, the grocer with a few deft twists of his hand produced from a square of blue paper. This conical pack was the universal form of package before the advent of the paper bag. It was versatile and accommodating. It fitted into any sized hand: nip off the end and one had a funnel to pour the contents into the narrowest of necked bottles. Should one forget the jar or jug, it was leak-proof enough to hold thick black treacle or jam, provided it was held vertically until reaching home.

The certainty of receiving samples of the mouth-watering stock was another reason for my eagerness to accompany Mother on this shopping expedition. A snippet of cheese, a broken biscuit from the tin of the variety Mother had chosen, a few currants, a raisin or a loose date from the compressed block of them on the counter, were the usual titbits offered. But best of all was a piece of crystallised sugar from the candied peel of oranges and lemons, their colours brightening the shop and heralding the approach of Christmas with the promise of other seasonal sugary delights.

The Co-op

I cannot remember when, or why Mother ceased to buy her groceries at the crowded aromatic corner shop, but I have memories of shopping with her at the newer purpose-built Co-op store, where the main attraction for me was the overhead railway from counter to cash desk. By depressing a lever at the counter end, bill and money in a wooden holder were released and whisked by a spring-loaded mechanism to the counting-house, the cashier returning the receipted bill and change in the same manner. There were no sacks or bins in this clinically clean and uncluttered shop. Tea and sugar, rice and currants were pre-packed in brightly coloured tins and cartons, and stacked in orderly rows on spotless shelves. The treacle was no longer loose and black, but tightly tinned and golden. Dairy produce, cheese and bacon, was under glass and, no longer exposed to the air, was unable to scent the shop with that mixture of aromas of farm produce that once pervaded every grocer's shop.

Its granolithic floor had no undulations or the unevenness of a wooden one that had been worn by countless feet of generations of customers. There were no cracks or crevices in its surface, nor was it sanded or sawdusted as was the custom of grocers, butchers and general store owners of those days. Its mopped and polished surface and the glazed tiled walls reflected the harsh light of the electric bulbs suspended from the glossy white ceiling. The smoky oil lamps and the hissing, flickering gas-jets, which in the older shops deepened the darkness of their already dim corners, had given way to this new brash brightness. All was haste and bustle.

There were no chairs on which to sit and watch expectantly the assembly of the order, for no currant, raisin or date escaped its cardboard pack. The pleasure and the fun of shopping had gone. Maybe I was growing up. The aerial railway was no longer an attraction, and my regular shopping excursions with Mother became an occasional errand to fetch some item omitted from the weekly order.

9

FROM SCHOOL TO
THE CARPENTERS' SHOP

The end of my schooldays

The rosy hue that tinged the eastern sky was fading and the warming sun, now free of the Downs, had dispersed the early morning mists of the marsh and of the low-lying fields in the valley below. Only a few wisps remained, outlining the meanderings of the river through the water meadows to the north, the east and to the south of the ancient red-roofed town.

From my eyrie above the sheer chalk cliff, reached that morning by walking and running up the long but gentle grassy slope from the outskirts of the town, I looked out and down upon my childhood's world of wonder and adventure. On that May morning in 1923 I had risen earlier than usual and with Nell, my brown smooth-coated terrier, had jogged through the sleepy street and up the hill path to my vantage point where, as on many another morning, I sat regaining my breath before returning, with body glowing, to devour the breakfast that awaited me. Below me the damp, low-lying ground, criss-crossed by kingcupped brooks, stretched away to the river and beyond. I gazed down on fields and meadows where in a few short weeks the corn and hay would ripple in the breeze. I saw woods and hedgerows and twisting lanes disappearing into the distance, until the vast green and brown tapestry of the Weald merged with the blue grey of the morning sky.

Little had changed in the centuries since, on another May morning, the fleeing Londoners of De Montfort's army were slaughtered by Prince Edward's knights in the water meadows below. The marsh which trapped and the river which drowned them, in their panic to reach the sanctuary of the church on its low hill amid the flood plain, are still as treacherous. No other buildings remain of the community the church once served. A farm, old but not of that era, is the only habitation within a mile of the asylum the doomed men had hoped to reach. The church stands alone on its knoll, now an island, surrounded by river and canal. The old river still guards three sides, but a canal has been cut on the fourth to bypass the river's meander and so shorten and ease a barge's journey from the inland brickfields and sawmills to the town or coast.

The old road still clings to the hillside and follows its contours. Once rough and rutted, muddy in winter and dusty in summer, its surface is now smooth, tarred and sanded. But the greatest change on that checkerboard of wood and meadow, brook and river, has been the advent of the railway. It bursts upon the scene from a cutting in the higher ground to the north. Over level crossing, and on embankment and bridge, it aims its steel shaft at the very heart of the old town. Perched on their chalky hill, town and castle defied its assault, forcing it to burrow deep beneath, to emerge on the southern side, leaving their flinty walls unbreached. Like an arrow, the track pointed to the town where I was born and where, on the morrow, in a building nestling against these castle walls, I was to start work.

My father was a builder, carrying on the business started by my grandfather in the latter half of the nineteenth century. From the first small workshop in the garden of his house, my father developed the business and enlarged the premises. A stable and yard adjoining – bought for £110 – were converted and adapted to house the bricklayers' equipment and materials. A short distance away, in a building with a sagging red-tiled roof, and built against the outer face of the castle wall, with flints and chalk blocks no doubt salvaged from demolished portions, the white-aproned carpenters practised their craft, and the painters mixed and matched the tints of their trade. Here tomorrow I was to start my apprenticeship, guided and encouraged by the kindly senior carpenter.

The carpenters' shop

The L-shaped, white-walled building lay against the castle wall. The shorter side pierced an ancient breach, its end against the base of the towering kilns of a malthouse built within the castle precincts. The entrance to the carpenters' shop was at the kiln end of this short side. A wide, ledged and braced matchboarded door opened into a narrow yard, where timber stacked on beams and ladders racked on walls were protected from the weather by a tiled lean-to roof.

It became my responsibility to unlock the yard and workshop doors each morning at six o'clock, except for a short period during the depths of winter, when a later start was made. It was an eerie experience to hear and feel the men moving in the dim half-light of the unlit shop, preparing for their day's tasks. Selecting tools by touch and loading hand trucks with timber wrought the day before, ready to start the haul through the hilly streets of the town, and sometimes to the villages beyond, the moment the hazy outlines strengthened in the sunless, silent streets.

Since I was a child I have had the ability to wake at a given time, and have not had to rely on an alarm to arouse me of a morning. On occasions I have set a clock should my own inborn one fail, but I invariably woke ahead of the hour and switched off the bell before its sharp, shrill sound could disturb other sleepers. It was no new experience or hardship to be up at such an hour, and it was with pride in my responsibility that I turned the massive key in the equally massive lock, to allow the men, some of whom had walked considerable distances, access to the yard, the bench and their tasks for the day.

Apart from being essential to operate the large lock of the yard door, there were no doubt sound practical reasons for a key of such huge proportions. It could not be overlooked or left behind. You were aware of its presence, or missed its weight. It might be mislaid but it could not be lost. A colossus of a key. Put it down and it would become an obstacle. Hanging on its hook it stood out among the ironmongery festooning the workshop wall but, fail to return it to its appointed place, the vacant expanse of white-washed wall signalled its absence. A heavyweight of the locksmith's craft, with elementary and simple wards, a collector's curio of character, worthy of any museum, where I hope it has now found rest.

The workshop was three wooden steps above the level of the yard, behind a scraped and scratched matchboarded door. The shop's patched, uneven wooden floor spanned what was once the castle moat, now a cellar dim and cool, storing the products of the brewery whose premises dominated the area, and whose brews twice a week perfumed the air with the heady scent of malt and hops. Half a dozen benches, their tops scored by generations of carpenters, stood in a wooden row on the shaving-littered floor. This pine-perfumed curly carpet kept one's feet warm in winter, and brought the scent of woodlands to the workshop on many a dismal day.

There were no motorised machines to ease the labours of the men. Planks and boards were ripped with saws and made smooth with planes, powered by muscled arms. Even the primitive circular saw was turned by hand. A short spell on this soon made one's arms and shoulders ache with the effort needed to maintain a uniform speed. The cold of the unheated shop in winter was not noticed after a few minutes turning of the heavy iron wheel, but in the heat of summer it was a task to avoid. The back-aching labour and sometimes tedious work were offset by jobs full of interest and variety. The carpenter was never bored. He had to use his intelligence throughout the long day. He was left to work things out for himself. He set out, cut, shaped, assembled and completed the work, often in primitive working conditions requiring great physical effort, with cheerfulness and pride. His counterpart in a modern mechanised shop, working at repetitive jobs, is more mentally weary, though less tired physically, than the craftsman working longer hours, fifty years ago.

EPILOGUE

"Before you put my book away
Remember me and maybe say
What fun that boy had yesterday"

August 3rd, 1978

AFTERWORD

by the editor

There must be many people in Lewes who still remember Mr Wells, who never lost contact with his native town. Other readers will surely want to know what happened to Mr Wells, whom we leave at the end of the book beginning his apprenticeship in his father's workshop.

When Mr Wells's father came back from the First World War, his own father had become resistant to any changes in the firm, and Mr Wells's father to some extent lost heart. Perhaps it was because the business was going into decline that Mr Wells went to work in the early 1930s for George Justice, cabinetmaker, where he is still remembered with great affection and respect. He then decided to take the City and Guilds Handicraft Examination in woodwork, with a view to teaching. He did this most successfully, setting up handicraft classes in schools throughout Sussex, after which he taught woodwork at what was then the Burgess Hill London Road School.

When war broke out in 1939 Mr Wells joined the R.A.F. His job was as a weapons inspector, to which he brought the sharp eye and meticulous precision that distinguished him in everything that he did: he reached the rank of acting wing commander. After the war he went back to the school in Burgess Hill, which later became Oakmeeds School. In 1959 he met his wife, who was also a teacher at the school, and they married in 1960.

Mr Wells taught at Oakmeeds until his retirement and spent the rest of his life in Burgess Hill. As well as writing this memoir he wrote poems, continued to do fine woodwork in his own workshop and traced his family tree back to the marriage of Richard Wells in 1640. The entire family since then has been born and bred in Sussex, chiefly in Wadhurst, Mayfield and Lewes.

THE FRIENDS OF LEWES SOCIETY

The Friends of Lewes Society is the civic society for Lewes and is affiliated to the Civic Trust and the Federation of Sussex Amenity Societies. The Society was formed in 1952 and since then has lobbied relevant bodies to maintain and improve the historical and environmental aspects of Lewes for the people who live in and visit the town. Over the years traffic has been a dominant issue, initially in fighting the proposed inner relief road which would have cut the town in two and more recently in supporting proposals for sustainable transport so that the problems caused by increased traffic are more tolerable.

The Society also strives to improve the physical appearance of the town and considers all planning applications, giving special consideration to those in the conservation area. It is supporting the inclusion of Lewes in the proposed South Downs national park. From its limited resources it has contributed to a number of projects in the town that have enhanced the streetscape or provided information for tourists. The Society has also published a number of books about Lewes.

With over 500 members, the Society's views are held in high regard by the various councils and other bodies it deals with. Often developers seek its views before formulating their proposals. Membership is open to all, and application forms can be obtained from the Town Hall. Members receive three newsletters and an annual report each year, as well as the opportunity to attend a number of events that have a bearing on the Society's objectives.

ALSO PUBLISHED BY
THE FRIENDS OF LEWES

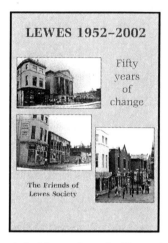

LEWES 1952–2002

Fifty years of change

The Friends of Lewes Society

LEWES **1952–2002: Fifty years of change**
Pomegranate Press; 96 pages; £8.95
ISBN 0 9542587 2 X
For anyone tempted to take the beautiful historic townscape of Lewes for granted this book will be an eye-opener. Those who care for the fabric and atmosphere of our county town have had to wage repeated battles in order to preserve its legacy of fine buildings and attractive open spaces.

The Friends of Lewes Society has been at the forefront of many such campaigns over the years. As a celebration of its first half-century it held a series of talks and meetings in the town, asking its speakers to peer into the future of Lewes as well as to evoke its recent past. Those lectures are reproduced in these pages, together with a fascinating collection of photographs and old picture postcards.